LUCKY CAT

T0364032

ISBN 978-0-7624-5944-5

Running Press Book Publishers
An Imprint of Perseus Books, LLC.,
A Subsidiary of Hachette Book Group, Inc.
2300 Chestnut Street
Philadelphia, PA 19103-4371

www.runningpress.com

CONTENTS

INTRODUCTION

If you have ever dined at a Japanese restaurant, shopped at an Asian supermarket, or wandered the streets of a Chinatown near you, you've probably noticed a cat figurine perched in a window or by the register. Modeled after the calico Japanese bobtail cat, Lucky Cat sits sentinel with an upright paw or two, beckoning customers and inviting good fortune.

This adorable ancient Japanese symbol of luck migrated from east to west. In its home country Japan, Lucky Cat is called *maneki-neko*, which means "beckoning hand." This can be confusing to the average Westerner, as the figurine appears to be waving. In Japan, holding the palm out with fingers folding up and down is actually a beckoning gesture.

This content cat is a shopkeeper's best friend, inviting customers inside with its alluring charms. A diverse array of colors, materials, and accessories contribute to the many Lucky Cats of the world, but no matter what, Lucky Cat is a welcome talisman.

LUCKY LORE

The true origins of Lucky Cat remain a mystery, but most will agree they first appeared during the Edo period in Japan, which lasted from the seventeenth century to mid-nineteenth century. A few legends weave a tale of the cat's birth, and three seem to stand the test of time.

The first legend has it that in the seventeenth century, there was an old dilapidated temple located west of Tokyo. A poor priest there had a cat named Tama, and he did his best to share his meager food with the cat. One day there was no food and the priest, on the verge of starvation, berated the cat for taking the little food he had while never contributing to the temple in any way. The cat walked outside as it began to rain. A wealthy samurai came riding by. He took shelter under a tree next o the temple and noticed Tama, who appeared to be beckoning him to come inside. His curiosity aroused, he followed Tama into the temple. Moments later, lightning struck the very tree he had been standing under. The samurai was so grateful to the cat for saving his life that he donated his riches to the temple, and when he passed away, a statue of the "lucky cat" that saved the samurai's life was made to celebrate his lifelong generosity.

Another story comes from an eighteenth

century geisha house. A popular courtesan named Usugumo had a pet cat that she loved dearly. One night as Usugumo was dressing, the cat began to tug on her kimono with urgency. The madam of the brothel saw this exchange and became convinced that the cat was possessed by an evil spirit. In haste, she chopped its head off with a sword! The head of the cat flew off and landed on a snake, which had poised to strike the geisha. The geisha was sad for the loss of her brave, beloved pet. A guest carved a cat statue out of wood to make her feel better, which she perched outside as an invitation to customers and as a reminder of the luck her favorite cat had brought her.

The last legend tells of a monk who lived in a shabby hut with his trusty cat. One day, a group of samurai warriors walked by the monk's meager home, and spotted his cat who appeared to be waving. Intrigued, they decided to come inside for a quick rest before their long journey home. As the monk served them tea, he preached to the samurai.

His words moved them to want to adopt the ways of the monk. One samurai exclaimed, "I am not just a samurai, but a king, King Ii Naotaka, and due to your cat's clever invitation inside, we were able to hear your holy words. It must be Buddha's will!" He and his compatriots immediately began drafting plans to turn the monk's modest home into a grand temple. The temple was named *Gotokuji*, "the cat temple."

DIVERSE KITTY

MANEKI MATERIAL

raditionally, these felines were carved
om wood, handmade with porcelain,
r even created out of durable cast iron.
oday's cats are usually made of ceramic.
he most intricate figurines are made
ut of jade or, in special cases, gold.

CAT COLOR

This happy cat can come in many color
each inviting its own special blessing int
the home or business it guards.

BLACK AND ORANGE beckons good luc
WHITE summons purity and happiness
BLACK prompts good health and ban
ishes evil spirits
GOLD inspires wealth and prosperity
GREEN OR BLUE bring academic succes
RED wards off illness
PINK invites love and romance

PAW POSITION

Next time you see a friendly Lucky Ca
in a restaurant window, pay attention
which paw is in the air? A left paw u
is meant to attract customers to bus
nesses like geisha houses and bar:
and a right paw in the air is meant t
beckon luck and wealth to any estab
lishment. Traditionally, most cats wer
modeled with just the left paw in th
air, but after the worldwide economi
downturn in 2008, figurines with bot
paws up became popular—peopl

wanted all the luck and protection they could get!

A few factors contribute to the height of the cat's paws. Some say the higher the paw, the greater the luck. Another belief is that the height of the paw corresponds to the direction good fortune will come from. If a cat has both hands up, you'll often see that one paw is higher than the other, so as not to be mistaken for a surrendering gesture.

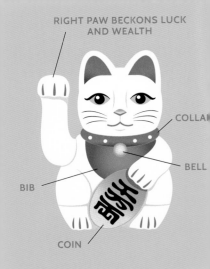

RIGHT PAW BECKONS LUCK AND WEALTH

COLLAR

BELL

BIB

COIN

ANCIENT ACCESSORIES

Bib, bell, collar, coin . . . what do a Lucky Cat's adornments tell us? In Japanese culture, objects tell stories and hold meaning. Lucky Cat's charms are not just decorative—each ornament plays its role in inviting wealth, banishing evil, or bringing good fortune.

COIN: Often these charming kitties wi be seen holding the valuable *koban* coi from Japan's Edo period. The coin wa worth one *ryou*, a great sum, and it said that when a Lucky Cat possesse a *koban*, it is worth ten million *ryou*. Lucky Cat clutching a coin invites wealt and material abundance.

BIB: Bibs were worn by cats in prosper ous homes during Japan's Edo period but Lucky Cat's bib may have a mor complex origin. Statues of the Buddhis deity *Jizo Bosatsu* are often found guarding Japanese holy sites like shrines and graveyards. When a child would recover from an illness, tradition dictated that the parents visit a *Jizo* statue and place a bib around its neck to show gratitude for the child's recovery. A Lucky Cat with a bib is also considered to ward off poor health.

COLLAR: In seventeenth century Japan, having a cat was considered a sign of wealth, as cats were very expensive. Affluent women would affectionately adorn their kitties with a collar dyed with *hichirimen*, a vibrant red flower.

BELL: Bells were used by prosperous owners to keep track of their cats. When a cat was out of sight, the owner could follow the faint sound of bells to retrieve her feline friend.

MALLET: *Daikoku Mantra*, the god of farmers, had a mallet that gold coins fell from when shaken. It is said that shaking Lucky Cat's mallet turns it into a magical money mallet, bringing wealth and prosperity.

CARP: These fish symbolize abundance, courage, and strength—for those are the qualities it takes for a carp to have the will and determination to spend its life swimming upstream.

MARBLE: These clear orbs represent crystal balls and invite wisdom and deep thought.

DOLL: The *daruma* doll is a Japanese wishing doll, which holds hope for good outcomes. Whether you are wishing to get a good grade on an exam or find a soulmate, the *daruma* will bring you auspicious luck. If a *daruma* has blank eyes,

paint one eye while making a wish. When
the wish comes true, paint the other eye
in celebration of your good fortune!

FRUIT AND VEGETABLES: A Lucky Cat holding a radish, gourd, or other bountiful fruit or vegetable is inviting a good harvest for the coming season.

FAMOUS FELINE

Lucky Cat is a world-famous character, appearing in films and televisioshows, and especially in video gameoriginating in Japan.

In the video game *Super Mario 3L World*, a bronze jingling bell transformMario into a Lucky Cat Mario! This giveMario the cat-like ability to scale walls bounce on enemies, scratch anyone in his path and speed into a lickety-split sprint. When Lucky Cat Mario crouches in mid-air and lands on his seat, he transforms into Golden Statue Mario—a shiny yellow cat who collects lucky gold coins! Mario's friends Luigi, Toad, Princess Peach, Rosalina, and Bowser can also become Lucky Cats with similar powers.

In the Pokémon games, the cream-colored, tan-footed Meowth has an oval gold coin embedded in its forehead. Sound familiar? The character is based on

Lucky Cat and his traditional *koban* coin

Some people attribute the fictional character Hello Kitty's origins to Lucky Cat. It is said that "Hello Kitty" may be a faulty translation of its Japanese name *maneki neko*.

CONCLUSION

For businesses seeking customers, prosperity, and good fortune, Lucky Cat is the cutest addition to a shop window. This welcoming feline summons bounty and beauty in the traditions of ancient Japan. Let Lucky Cat be your most loyal and patient pet and bring you good fortune each day!

This book has been bound using handcraft methods and Smyth-sewn to ensure durability.

Illustrated by Sneaky Raccoon.

Designed by Ashley Haag.

Written by Danielle Selber.

Edited by Cindy De La Hoz.

The text was set in Avenir, Cabin, and GB Shinto.